Great temples, shrines and Buddhist monuments were constructed as Buddhism provided the moral strength for defending the kingdom and unifying the peninsula.

As Shilla flourished, Kyŏngju, which was called various names including Saro, Sŏrabŏl, Kyerim and Kŭmsŏng, developed into one of the world's largest cities with a population estimated at about one million. In the middle of the city was the royal palace enclosed by a half moon-shaped earthen fortress, and in the outskirts were pavilions where the royal family and members of the court enjoyed banquets and picnics. It was at one of these pavilions that the kingdom virtually came to an end when, in 927, Kyŏngae-wang, its next to the last ruler, was forced to fall on his sword by a rebel leader seeking to restore the Paekche Kingdom.

The attack was the result of the decadence of the ruling class who had grown to ignore the welfare of the people and the nation as a whole. From around 900, rebel leaders such as the one who attacked Kyŏngae-wang tore Shilla apart and set up their own kingdoms, Latter Paekche and Latter Koguryŏ. In 934, Wang Kŏn, the leader of Latter Koguryŏ, attacked and defeated Latter Paekche and in 935 accepted the abdication of Kyŏngsun-wang, Shilla's last king. Such was the beginning of Koryŏ and the end of Shilla. Shortly thereafter, the ex-Shilla capital began to be called Kyŏngju in 940.

A bird's-eye view of Pulguksa Temple.

PULGUKSA

Built on a series of stone terraces, Pulguksa appears to emerge organically from the rocky terrain of the wooded foothills of Mt. T'ohamsan about 16 kilometers southeast of downtown Kyŏngju. This is because it was built in accordance with ancient notions of architecture and principles of geomancy that manmade structures should not be obtrusive but should harmonize with the surroundings. It is both monolithic and intricate and takes on different guises as the light and shadows shift and the weather changes.

The temple dates to a small temple Shilla's 23rd monarch, King Pŏphŭng (r. 514–540), had erected for his queen to pray for the prosperity and peace of the kingdom. However, its present structures date to 757 when Kim Tae-sŏng, the chief minister of the time, built the large "Temple of the Buddha Land." The stonework including the foundations, staircases, platforms and several pagodas date from that time, but the wooden edifices date to 1973

The imposing facade of Pulguksa with its mortarless bridges of stairs (left). One of several gates one must pass through to enter the temple (below), this one has a sign announcing the 2532nd anniversary of Buddha's birth.

when the temple was completely restored.

The temple's facade is dominated by two large mortarless stone balustraded staircases. The one on the right comprises a lower flight called Paegun-gyo (Bridge of White Clouds) and an upper flight called Ch'ŏng-un-gyo (Bridge of Azure Clouds) and the one on the left, two flights called Ch'ilbogyo (Seven Treasures Bridge) and Yŏnhwagyo (Lotus Bridge). They are called bridges because they symbolically lead from the secular world to Pulguk, the Land of the Buddha.

The "cloud bridge stairway" leads to Chahamun (Mauve Mist Gate), the main entrance to Taeungjŏn, the main sanctuary. The other staircase leads to Anyangmun (Pure Land Gate), the entrance to Kŭngnakchŏn, a secondary sanctum.

The "cloud bridge stairway" leads to Chahamun Gate, the main entrance to Taeungjŏn, the temple's main hall (below). At right is Haet'algyo, a bridge leading to Ch'ŏnwangmun, which houses four fierce looking Deva kings, including the guardians of the East and South (lower right), the protectors of Buddhism and Buddhist doctrine.

Although it is not Pulguksa's largest building, the colorful Taeungjŏn is certainly the most important, enshrining an image of Sakyamuni, the Historic Buddha. The gilt-bronze image made in 1765 is flanked by Dipamkara, the Bodhisattva of the Past, and Maitreya, the Bodhisattva of the Future, and two *arhats*, or disciples, Ananda and Kasyapa. Ananda, the younger of the two, is a cousin of Sakyamuni and his habitual attendant. Kasyapa is a leading disciple.

The building is decorated with colorful *tanch'ŏng* patterns which are not only a reflection of the Buddhist heaven but also an attempt to bring the harmony and unity of the cosmos to earth for man's easy access. Horned dragons look down from the eaves of the roof.

In the courtyard of Taeungjŏn are two of Korea's most beautiful pagodas: the 8.3-meter-high Sŏkkat'ap (Pagoda of Sakyamuni) and the 10.5-meter-high Tabot'ap (Many Treasures Pagoda), both built around 756. A mimicry of wood construction dominates the motifs of both pagodas. It is recorded that Kim Tae-sŏng had them built for his parents, which could be one reason the Sŏkkat'ap is rather masculine and the Tabot'ap feminine.

Kŭngnakchŏn (Hall of Great Bliss), to the left

Taeungjŏn, the main worship hall (below) in front of which is an 8th century, stone lantern. Paintings like this Buddha (right) adorn the woodwork under the eaves of the hall. An image of Sakyamuni (lower right) dominates the hall's altar.

After hundreds of years only one lion remains to guard the intricate Tabot'ap Pagoda which graces the courtyard of Taeungjŏn.

The simple lines of the Sŏkkat'ap Pagoda complement the elegant contours of the Tabot'ap. Legend says the beautiful pair were built by a stonemason from Paekche named Asadal.

This gilt-bronze Amitabha Buddha (left) dominates the altar of *Kŭngnakchŏn* (lower left) and this gilt-bronze Vairocana Buddha (right) dominates the altar in *Pirojŏn*. *Musŏlchŏn* (lower right), the temple's largest building, is a lecture hall.

of Taeungjŏn, enshrines a gilt bronze image of Amitabha, the Buddha of the Western Paradise. A masterpiece of Buddhist sculpture, the image is believed to have been made in 1750.

Behind Taeungjŏn is the temple's largest building, a 34.13-meter-long lecture hall called Musŏlchŏn. It is interesting to note that the name literally means no lecture which implies that truth cannot be obtained through lectures. Behind and to the left of this hall is Pirojŏn (Hall of Vairocana), where an imposing gilt-bronze image of Vairocana, the Buddha of All-pervading Light, made during the eighth or ninth century, is enshrined. The mudra, or hand gesture of this image, symbolizes that the multitude and the Buddha are one. To the right of Pirojŏn is Kwanŭmjŏn in which an image of Avalokitesvara, the Bodhisattva of Mercy is enshrined. The image was made when the temple was restored.

This is part of a covered corridor that extends from the left and right of the Chahamun and Anyangmun gates and connects Taeungjŏn, Kŭngnakchŏn and Musŏlchŏn (below). Tanch'ŏng patterns emblazon the eaves of Kŭngnakchŏn (right).

16

This mortarless stone wall (below) supports part of the corridor that connects Taeungjŏn, Kŭngnakchŏn and Musŏlchŏn. Kyŏngnu and Pŏmyŏngnu, pavilions at the front corners of the corridor, contain this wooden fish and drum (right) and several other musical instruments used in various ceremonies.

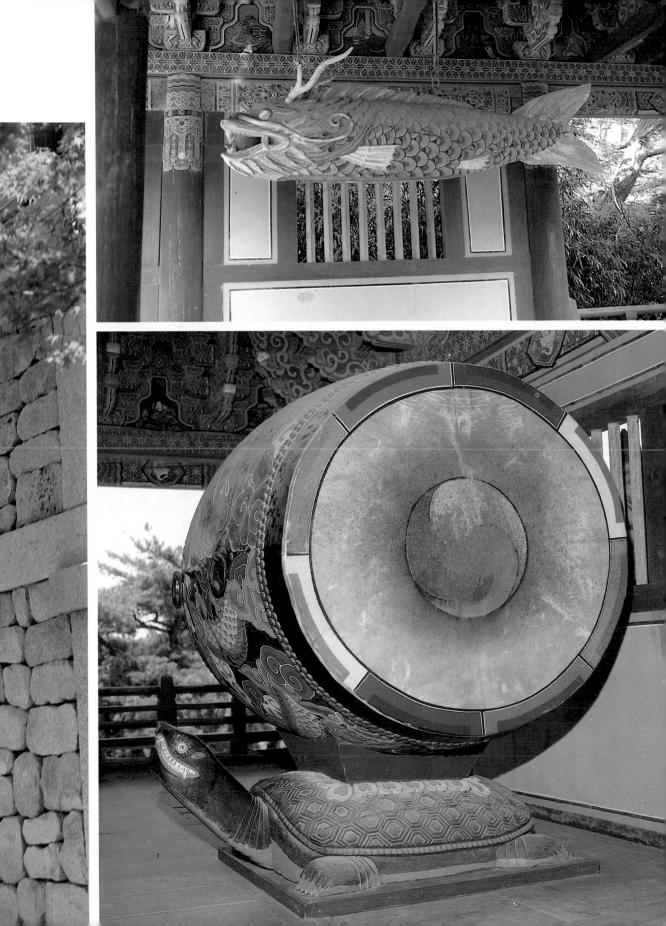

Buddhist monks and laymen listen to a lecture at Pulgukkangwon, an institution for teaching sutras established at Pulguksa in 1978 (below). At the bottom is an intricately carved stupa near Pirojŏn called Kwanghakpudo and a grouping of stupas located on the grounds of the temple.

SŎKKURAM

High up on the mountain behind Pulguksa is Sŏkkuram, a manmade stone grotto designed around the worship of a principal statue of Buddha. One of Asia's finest Buddhist grottos, it is a reflection of the application of advanced scientific principles and precise mathematical and architectural concepts, not to mention great technical skills.

Supposedly built in the eighth century by Kim Tae-sŏng, the architect of Pulguksa, it comprises a square antechamber and a round interior chamber with a domed ceiling connected by a rectangular passageway. In addition to a large image of a seated Buddha in the rotunda, it has 37 figures, mostly in high relief, arranged according to their functions and ranks in the Buddhist pantheon. Many of them are protectors of the main chamber in which the principal statue of Buddha is seated facing the east.

The mountain ridge where the manmade Sŏkkuram grotto shrine is located commands a panoramic view of the valley where Pulguksa is located. The wood and tile structure protects the entrance to the grotto.

The Buddha image (left) in the rotunda of Sŏkkuram is considered by many art historians to be the most perfect Buddhist statue in the world. However, its identity is controversial; some say it is Sakyamuni, the Historic Buddha, while others say it is Amitabha, the Buddha of the Western Paradise. It is placed in the rotunda in such a way that the first rays of the sun rising over the East Sea strike the urna, the jewel in the forehead. These are two of the four Bodhisattvas (below) that stand in attendance of the Buddha on either side of the pillars just inside the rotunda.

Sunrise at Sŏkkuram: The undulating sweep of mountains looks like a distant sea.

TAEWANGAM

Among the most beautiful and interesting sites in and around Kyŏngju is Taewangam, the underwater tomb of King Munmu-wang (r.661-681). Munmu-wang succeeded Muyŏl-wang (r.654-661), who defeated Paekche in alliance with T'ang China in 660. He completed the unification of the Korean peninsula by defeating Koguryŏ in 668 and driving the T'ang Chinese forces out of the country.

Munmu-wang asked that upon his death his body would be cremated in a simple funeral and also expressed the wish that he be re-incarnated as a dragon so that he could defend Shilla from invaders. His body was thus cremated and the remains are believed to have been either buried under these rocks (below) or strewn over them. The rocks, which are known as the Great King's Rocks, are 19.8 meters from shore.

Taewangam is the only known underwater tomb in the world.

TUMULI PARK

Since Kyŏngju was home to 56 Shilla kings and queens, it is only natural that its cityscape and environs are punctuated with massive royal tombs. The most visible are the 20 grass-covered mounds of varying size that make up what is called Tumuli Park. The 152,000-square-meter park was like any other neighborhood until it was cleared of homesites and the tombs rehabilitated and landscaped in a restoration project that began in 1973.

At that time several tombs including a large two-mound one called Hwangnamdaech'ong were excavated. An inscription on a silver girdle excavated from one of the mounds of

Tumuli Park (below).
Stone figures of civilian and military officials guard Kwaenŭng (left), thought to be the tomb of Wonsŏng-wang (r.785-798). This unusual 13-story, 9th century pagoda (lower left) marks the site of an ancient temple called Chŏnghyesa while it is not known to which temple this pagoda (lower right) belonged.

Hwangnamdaech'ong showed it to be the tomb of a Shilla queen, although her name is not known.

However, it was the excavations of what has become known as Ch'ŏnmach'ong, or "Heavenly Horse Tomb," that proved the most enlightening. More than ten thousand objects were excavated from the tomb. They included an exquisite gold foil crown with jade pendants, a gold crown cup and ornaments, a long gold belt with dangling jade and gold ornaments, bracelets, ear pendants, and bronze and ceramic funerary items not to mention a birch bark saddle piece painted with a flying horse from which the name of the unidentified tomb was derived. The tomb has been turned into a museum with a replica of the burial chamber and reproductions of some of the burial items. The original relics are displayed in the National Museums in Seoul and Kyŏngju.

The only tomb to be identified in the park is that of Mich'u-wang (r. 261-284), the 13th ruler of Shilla and the first of the Kim clan. It has traditionally been called Chukhyŏnnŭng, meaning Bamboo Tomb, because, according to legend, a strange army of men with bamboo leaves in their ears appeared and helped Shilla win a major battle and then disappeared in front of the tomb. From that time, the spirit of the king is said to have been worshipped by Shilla as the protector of the kingdom.

Tourists can go inside Ch'ŏnmach'ong, the Heavenly Horse Tomb, to see a replica of the burial chamber (below). The tomb is called Ch'ŏnmach'ong for this birch bark saddle piece (upper right) which was excavated from it along with this saddle, stirrups and other tack (lower right).

This gold and jade crown, gold girdle with dangling ornaments, gold crown ornaments and bronze funerary vessels (clockwise from left) were all excavated from Ch'ŏnmach'ong.

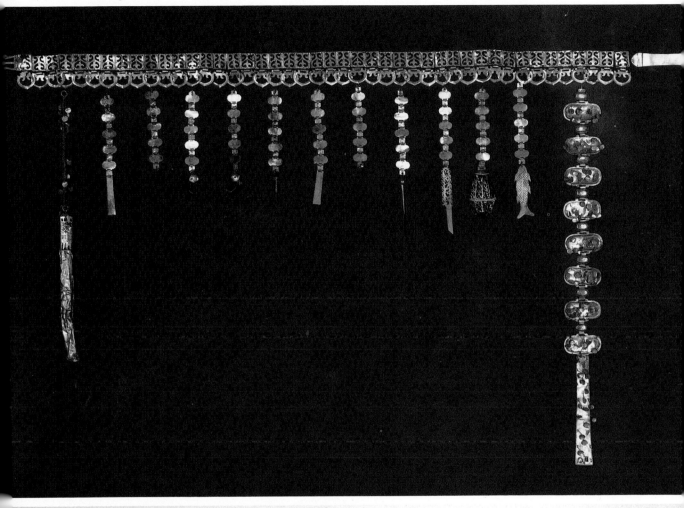

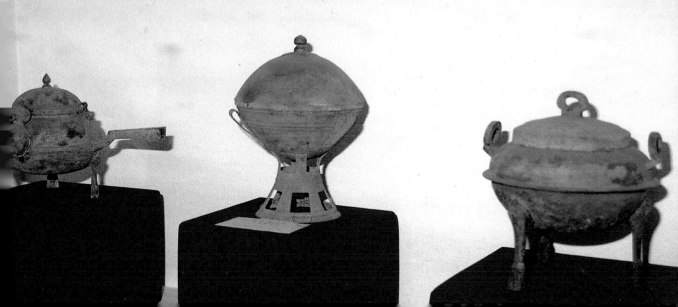

HISTORIC SITES AND MONUMENTS

Located within Kyŏngju City and its out-skirts are a number of historic sites and monuments. These include a number of tombs, pagodas, shrines, palace sites, an observatory, a forest, a "sacred mountain," and more, all of which are within a short distance of the Kyŏngju National Museum.

Two of Kyŏngju's oldest and most interesting structures are Punhwangsat'ap Pagoda and Ch'ŏmsŏngdae Observatory, both built during the reign of Queen Sŏndŏk-yŏwang (r.632–647), Shilla's 27th ruler.

The three-story Punhwangsat'ap stands on the grounds of Punhwangsa Temple which was constructed in 634. Made of stones carved to resemble bricks, it is believed to have been originally seven or nine stories high.

The bottle-shaped Ch'ŏmsŏngdae is considered the oldest observatory in Asia. Korea's oldest secular structure, it is especially intriguing in that it is made of 362 stones, the number of days in a lunar calendar year, and there are 12 rectangular base stones and 12 rectangular stones above and below a window in the side, which could correspond to the number of months of the year and the number of animals of the Oriental zodiac.

Punhwangsat'ap was constructed in imitation. of earlier wooden pagodas.

Ch'ŏmsŏngdae was used by Shilla astronomers to study the stars.

Panwolsŏng (top) is an earthen fortress where the Shilla palace was located. Sŏkpinggo (bottom), an ice storage, is one of the few relics that mark the site of the palace. Though restored many times, it was possibly constructed in the fourth century as it is recorded in the ancient Samguk sagi (History of the Three Kingdoms) that King Chijŭng-wang (r.500-514) had a stone ice storage built on the palace grounds in the sixth year of his reign.

Anapchi (top), originally made in 674, is a beautifully landscaped pond which was part of a garden of a detached palace. Foundation stones (bottom) mark the site of Hwangnyongsa, Shilla's largest temple which was built between 554 and 569. The temple site and Anapchi are both located in the eastern outskirts of Kyŏngju not far from Panwolsŏng.

O-NŬNG AND KYERIM

O-nŭng, or Five Tombs, are believed to be the tombs of Pak Hyŏkkŏse, the founder of Shilla and the Pak clan of Kyŏngju, his queen, and Namhae, Yuri, and P'asa, the second, third, and fifth kings of Shilla, respectively, although the tombs have never been excavated. South of the tombs is Sungdŏkchŏn, a shrine to King Hyŏkkŏse.

Kyerim, or Chicken Forest, is the birthplace of Kim Alchi, the founder of the Kyŏngju Kim clan to which most of Korea's Kims belong. It is called Chicken Forest because, according to legend, Shilla's King T'alhae (r.57–80) heard a cock crowing in the forest and sent an official to investigate who returned reporting that a white chicken was found under a gold box hanging from a tree. The king went to the forest and found the box contained a baby boy. He declared him his son and crown prince and gave him the surname Kim, which is written with the Chinese character for gold because the box was gold and the name Alchi.

Kyerim Forest, the legendary birthplace of Kim Alchi (below). The undulating mounds of O-nŭng (right), which includes the tomb of Shilla's founder-king Pak Hyŏkkŏse, and Sungdŏkchŏn (lower right), a shrine to him.

The Ch'oe Mansion (top), one of several ancient houses in a village in Kyŏngju, and the Kyŏngju Hyanggyo, a Confucian shrine-academy first established in 682 and restored in 1982.

KYŎNGJU NATIONAL MUSEUM

The Kyŏngju National Museum dates to 1913 when the Kyŏngju Historical Association renovated a Chosŏn-period guest house into a display hall for relics. The present facilities were constructed in 1975.

There are more than 40,000 relics including 14 National Treasures and 27 Treasures in the buildings and scattered about the grounds of the 68,000-square-meter compound. The galleries in the main building display prehistoric artifacts, relics from the early years of the Three Kingdoms period, many showing the influence of shamanism, beautifully decorated clay tiles and bricks, Buddhist statuary, ceramics, various metalcrafts and more. Relics recovered from tombs such as crowns, necklaces and other personal ornaments, parts of gilt-bronze armor and various funerary items are dispalyed in Annex I. Some of the more than 30,000 relics from Anapchi Pond such as a wooden boat, inscribed wooden tablets, Buddhist plaquettes, dice for playing a drinking game, and gilt-bronze bowls and other vessels which shed much light on the lifestyles of Shilla royalty are displayed in Annex II.

The Divine Bell of the Great King Sŏngdŏk, or Emille Bell, which is 3.07 meters high, 2.3 meters in diameter and weighs 23 tons, is displayed in a pavilion.

Reproductions of the Sŏkkat'ap and Tabot'ap pagodas and the remains of ancient pagodas, stupas, Buddhas and other relics grace the grounds of the Kyŏngju National Museum.

Ceramic funerary items are displayed in the second (left) and sixth (below) galleries, while stone Buddhas and Bodhisattvas, lions and other beasts are displayed in the eighth gallery (lower left). The 10.2-meter-high Kosŏnsat'ap (bottom), Korea's largest padoda, dominates the backyard of the Museum. It was moved from the site of Kosŏnsa Temple because of the construction of a dam.

ROYAL TOMBS

Three of the most interesting tombs in terms of their settings and occupants are the tombs of kings T'alhae, Muyŏl and Shinmun.

The tomb of T'alhae-wang (r. 57-58), Shilla's fourth ruler, is in a grove of gnarled pine trees. It is rather simple for a royal tomb. There is an interesting legend about this king who was the beginning of the Sŏk clan of Kyŏngju which produced seven Shilla kings. A queen of a faraway country gave birth to a large egg after a seven-year pregnancy. Thinking it must be something bad, she wrapped it in silk, put it in a wooden box and sent it out to sea. The box washed ashore in Korea where it was found by an old woman who opened it to find a handsome baby boy. She named him Sŏk after one of the Chinese characters comprising the word for magpie because magpies flew about cawing when she opened the box. He grew to be a bright, handsome, exceptionally large man. When King Namhae-wang heard of him, he married him to his first daughter. He eventually

The Divine Bell of the Great King Sŏngdŏk, cast in 770, hangs in a pavilion on the Museum grounds. It takes its popular name, Emille Bell, from an ancient Shilla word pronounced "em-ee-leh," which, according to legend, is what it sounded like when it was first rung (left).
This simple mound is the tomb of T'alhae-wang (r.57-80), the fourth king of Shilla and the first Shilla ruler to come from the Sŏk clan (below).

inherited the throne from Yuri-wang, the first son of Namhae and third ruler of Shilla, to become T'alhae-wang, T'alhae meaning to come out of a box after the cords are untied.

The tomb of Muyŏl-wang (r. 654–661), Shilla's 29th monarch, is in a pine forest at the foot of Sŏndosan. It is one of the largest tombs in Kyŏngju and thus befitting one of Shilla's greatest rulers. He first rose to fame as General Kim Ch'un-ch'u and, with the assistance of General Kim Yu-shin, a friend from childhood, managed to succeed Queen Chindŏk-yŏwang. He defeated Paekche in alliance with T'ang China in 660, thus paving the way for his son, King Munmu-wang to unify the peninsula by defeating Koguryŏ. The base of the tumulus is reinforced with natural stones.

Shinmun-wang (r. 681–692), Shilla's 31st ruler and the eldest son of Munmu-wang, set the stage for the golden age of the eighth century

At left is Nŭngjit'ap, all that remains of what is believed to have been a five-story pagoda and below is a base and a capstone, all that remain of a stele to the tomb of Muyŏl-wang (r. 654-661) (lower left).

The entrance (top) to the tomb of Shinmun-wang (r.681-692) whose enlightened rule led to the golden era of Unified Shilla (bottom).

These flagpole supports, a stele base and some foundation stones (top) are all that remain of Sach'ŏnwangsa Temple which was built in 679 in supplication of Buddha's protection against T'ang China. The 8th century triad is all that remains of Kulbulsa Temple (bottom).

by establishing absolutism, improving the system of government, promoting scholarship, increasing diplomatic relations with other countries and establishing a national educational institution to train future leaders. His tomb is a short distance from the site of Sach'ŏnwangsa Temple.

These are two of the zodiac panels (upper right) that encircle the tomb of General Kim Yu-shin (lower right), a former hwarang who helped defeat Koguryŏ, helped Kim Ch'un-ch'u ascend to the throne to become Muyŏl-wang (r.654–661) and then helped unify the peninsula by defeating Paekche and driving out the T'ang Chinese forces. He was posthumously given the title of Hŭngmu-daewang, meaning Great King Hŭngmu.

These three-story pagodas in Ch'ŏn-gun-ri mark the site of an ancient temple which was excavated in 1939 when they were restored. The name of the temple is unknown but the pagodas are thought to date from the second half of the 8th century.(below)

NAMSAN

About 4 kilometers south of downtown Kyŏngju is Namsan Mountain which is said to give up a relic with almost every turn of a shovel. It is sometimes called Kŭmosan, the "Mountain of the Golden Turtle," because it resembles a turtle facing the East Sea.

The "sacred mountain" is recorded to have had as many as 808 temples during Unified Shilla and even now its 35 legend-laden valleys are dotted with more than 300 historic sites and Buddhist relics and sculptures. There are also many tombs on its lower slopes.

An ancient fortress, Sŏch'ulchi, a pond from which legend says a letter came informing King Soji-wang (r.479–500) of a conspiracy, the remains of Shininsa Temple, a beautiful image

Sŏch'ulchi (below), a pond with legends which date to Shilla and a pavilion which dates to the Chosŏn Kingdom.
Yangsanjae (right) is a shrine built in 1970 to the six tribal chiefs who formed Shilla by making Pak Hyŏkkŏse their leader in 57 B.C. The stele (lower right) is to the Najŏng Well where Pak Hyŏkkŏse is said to have been born from an egg.

This tree and stones (left) and the abalone-shaped stone channel through which wine cups were floated (below) are the remains of P'osŏkchŏng, a summer pavilion where Kyŏngae-wang died at the hands of a rebel leader trying to restore the Paekche Kingdom.

At right is Samnŭng, the tombs of Adalla-wang (r.154-184), Shindŏk-wang (r.912-917) and Kyŏngmyŏng-wang (r.917-924), the 8th, 53rd and 54th rulers of Shilla, and at the lower right is the tomb of Chŏnggang-wang (r.886-887), who turned the throne over to his sister Chinsŏng-yŏwang (r.887-897) because of illness.

called the Porisa Buddha, P'osŏkchŏng, the site of a pavilion where King Kyŏngae-wang (r.924–927) met a tragic death at the hands of Kyŏnhwon, a general of Latter Paekche, that hastened the end of Shilla, and Ch'ilburam, seven Buddhist images, are among the interesting sites on its eastern slopes. Najŏng Well, where Shilla's first king, Pak Hyŏkkŏse, appeared in a bright egg, Yangsanjae, a shrine to the chief of the six tribes that formed Shilla

This, the largest cluster of relief carvings in Korea, 29 in all, is all that remains of a temple which was called Shininsa.

This 8th century image of Bhaisajyaguru, the Buddha of Medicine, at the site of Porisa Temple, is the best preserved Unified Shilla image in Namsan. Of special note are the Buddhas carved on the front and back of the halo (right). These images in Pae-dong (below), two Bodhisattvas and a Buddha, were found scattered about the slopes of Namsan and moved here in 1923. They are representative of 7th century Shilla sculpture.

by making Pak their king, and the Sambulsa Triad are just a few of the spots of interest on the western slopes of Namsan.

Among the more modern attractions on the slopes of Namsan are the Hwarang House built in 1973 and T'ongilchŏn (Unification Hall) built in 1977. The Hwarang House is an education center dedicated to promoting the ideals that guided Shilla's *hwarang,* an elite corps of young men trained in martial arts and imbued with a great sense of nationalism. The T'ongilchŏn is a memorial to King Muyŏl-wang, King Munmu-wang and General Kim Yu-shin, the three men most responsible for unifying the Korean peninsula under one rule.

The main hall of T'ongilchŏn where portraits of Muyŏl-wang, Munmu-wang and General Kim Yu-shin are enshrined (below). Steles to the three and a statue of Kim Yu-shin on horseback are among the monuments on the grounds of the hall (opposite : lower left and right). At right is a hall in the Hwarang House.

POMUN LAKE RESORT

Just 8.3 kilometers northeast of Kyŏngju City is what is perhaps Korea's most complete resort complex. Pomun Lake Resort, as the 1,045-hectare complex is called, is the creation of the Korean National Tourism Corporation. It is named for Pomun Lake, a 150-hectare lake that was made from an ancient pond.

The resort, which is easily accessible to Kyŏngju's historic sites, includes several deluxe hotels, a number of Korean-style inns, a well-equipped convention center large enough for international meetings, a large shopping center, several golf courses and a marina, all designed to combine Shilla architectural styling with the demands of modern facilities.

Paddle boats, sail boats, and row boats can be rented at the Pomun Lake Marina, where cruises are also available on large "swan" boats. Tennis, swimming, cycling and hiking are also available. Locally produced souvenirs and handicraft items can be purchased in the shopping center.

Located at the southern end of Pomun Lake Resort is Tot'urak World. It has camping sites, a swimming pool with a large slide, a soccer field, a baseball field and tennis courts. It also has an amusement park with a dream house and a number of carnival rides such as a ferris wheel, revolving motorcycles, sports cars and space fighters.

There are also food stands, restaurants and souvenir shops as well as a large parking lot.

A bird's-eye view of Pomun Lake Resort (below). Sailboats as well as row boats and motor boats can be enjoyed on the lake (right). A pagoda rises above some of the tiled-roof structures of the shopping and dining area (lower right).

Condominiums and deluxe hotels are among the accommodations the resort, which even has a botanical garden, offers. They are just a few minutes' walk from the convention center (left).

Souvenir shops, many selling items inspired by Shilla culture, abound in the Pomun Lake Resort as well as in the lodging area at Pulguksa Temple. Many shops specialize in ceramics produced at kilns in the Kyŏngju area.

KYŎNGJU FOLK CRAFT VILLAGE

Located on a 66,000-square-meter tract of land at the base of T'ohamsan is the Kyŏngju Folk Craft Village which was established to carry on, preserve and further develop traditional Korean folk arts and crafts and to promote both domestic and international understanding of Korea's cultural heritage.

Artisans and craftsmen from throughout the Kyŏngju area have moved into the village, which is a kind of cooperative, and live in traditional style houses. In their workshops they produce Shilla gold crowns, Buddhist statues, cloisonne and other metalcrafts, celadon, white porcelain, earthenware and other ceramics, woodcrafts, embroidery, bambooware and more. Visitors can visit their workshops to see them work and can see and purchase their finished products in the exhibition center.

Located at the foot of Mt. T'ohamsan is the Kyŏngju Folk Craft Village where handicrafts can be purchased (below).
The Tot'urak World at the southern end of Pomun Lake Resort (left) has something to please people of all ages from athletic facilities to carnival rides.

At left is an exhibition hall in the Kyŏngju Folk Craft Village. The village's workshops are open to the pubilc so that artisans like the woodcarver and ceramicist pictured here can be observed at work.

KYŎNGJU CITY

Kyŏngju is a small city with a population of about one hundred and forty thousand. Because of its many historic sites and monuments, industry is restricted in the city and its surroundings. The major sources of income are farming and tourism.

Among the shops that line the downtown streets are stores dealing in antiques, ceramics, paintings, calligraphy and all sorts of curios. There is also a traditional market.

Nightclubs of all sizes and descriptions can be found in the entertainment district, which is only a few blocks from the railroad station. The city also has many good restaurants. One of the best local specialties is *pŏpchu,* a delicious wine made of rice and herbs which, according to legend, was first brewed in Buddhist temples during Shilla.

Kyŏngju is easily accessible by train or bus from Seoul and many travel agencies offer package Kyŏngju trips including transportation and overnight accommodations.

This is one of the major streets in downtown Kyŏngju.

At left is an entrance to a traditional market in downtown Kyŏngju and the Kyŏngju Tourist Bus Terminal (lower left). Along the quieter city streets can be found private homes like these traditional ones with tile and thatch roofs (below).

SHILLA CULTURAL FESTIVAL

Every year in early October, when the fields around Kyŏngju are golden, the Shilla Cultural Festival, or Shilla Munhwaje as it is called in Korean, is held. It is to recall the great spirit of the Shilla people who unified the Korean peninsula under one rule and their great culture.

It begins with colorful rites honoring the god of heaven and includes various processions with floats, many illustrating Shilla legends, performing arts programs such as *nong-ak,* or farmers' music and dance, and *"Hwarangmu,"* a dance inspired by the *hwarang,* and traditional games such as *ch'ajŏn nori,* a game in which two teams compete to "dethrone" the other's leader who rides a large wooden chariot carried on the shoulders of the team members. There are also academic programs such as symposiums and seminars on Shilla culture and history.

Various organizations, neighborhood associations and schools participate in the Shilla Cultural Festival. Dressed in Shilla costumes, the participants enact Shilla legends, play traditional games, and perform traditional music and dance.

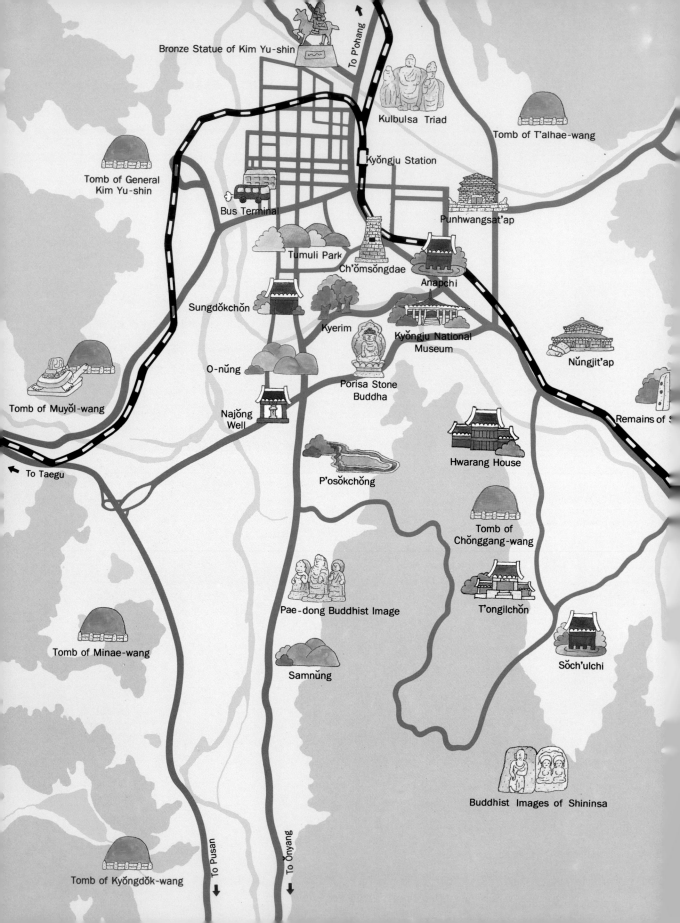

Bronze Statue of Kim Yu-shin

To P'ohang

Kulbulsa Triad

Tomb of T'alhae-wang

Kyŏngju Station

Tomb of General Kim Yu-shin

Bus Terminal

Punhwangsat'ap

Tumuli Park

Ch'ŏmsŏngdae

Anapchi

Sungdŏkchŏn

Kyerim

Kyŏngju National Museum

Nŭngjit'ap

O-nŭng

Porisa Stone Buddha

Tomb of Muyŏl-wang

Remains of S

Najŏng Well

To Taegu

P'osŏkchŏng

Hwarang House

Tomb of Chŏnggang-wang

Pae-dong Buddhist Image

T'ongilchŏn

Tomb of Minae-wang

Sŏch'ulchi

Samnŭng

Buddhist Images of Shininsa

Tomb of Kyŏngdŏk-wang

To Pusan

To Ŏnyang

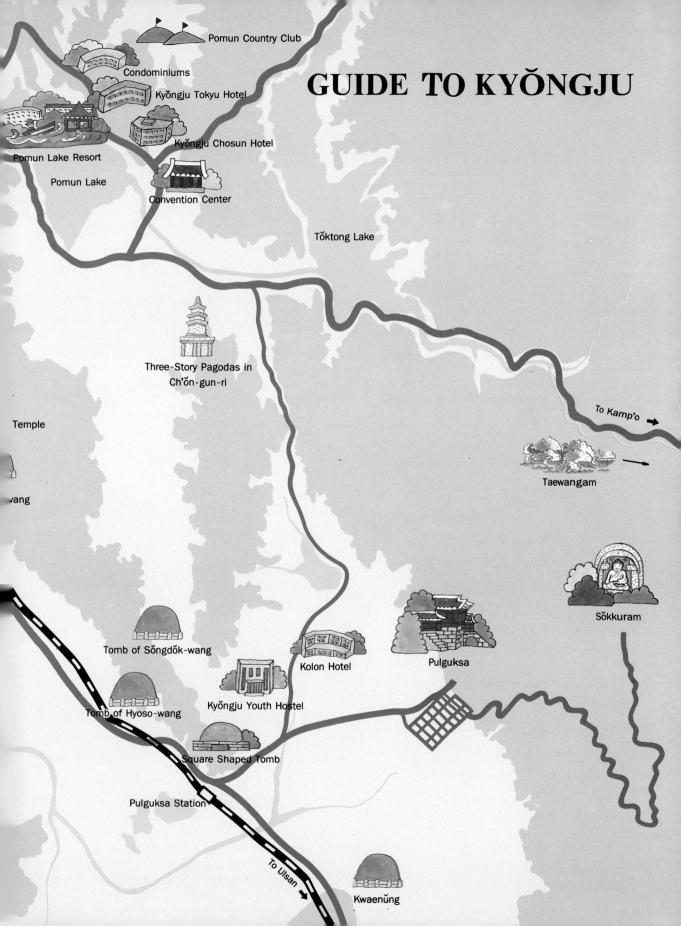

GUIDE TO KYŎNGJU

Pomun Country Club

Condominiums

Kyŏngju Tokyu Hotel

Kyŏngju Chosun Hotel

Pomun Lake Resort

Pomun Lake

Convention Center

Tŏktong Lake

Three-Story Pagodas in Ch'ŏn-gun-ri

To Kamp'o →

Temple

wang

Taewangam

Sŏkkuram

Tomb of Sŏngdŏk-wang

Kolon Hotel

Pulguksa

Tomb of Hyoso-wang

Kyŏngju Youth Hostel

Square Shaped Tomb

Pulguksa Station

To Ulsan →

Kwaenŭng

● Greetings

안녕하세요 ?
Annyŏnghaseyo ?

Good morning.

네, 안녕하세요 ?
Ne, annyŏnghaseyo ?

Good morning.

반갑습니다.
Pangapssŭmnida.

Pleased to meet you.

또 뵙겠어요.
Tto poepkessŏyo.

See you again.

안녕히 가세요.
Annyŏnghi kaseyo.

Good bye. (said to the person leaving)

안녕히 계세요.
Annyŏnghi keseyo.

Good bye. (said to the preson staying as you leave)

어떠십니까 ?
Ŏttŏshimnikka ?

How are you ?

요즘 바쁘십니까 ?
Yojŭm pappŭshimnikka ?

Are you busy lately ?

좋습니다. 감사합니다.
Chossŭmnida. Kamsahamnida.

Fine. Thank you.

안녕히 주무십시오.
Annyŏnghi chumushipshio.

Good night.

● Introduction

성함이 무엇이죠 ?
Sŏnghami muŏshijyo ?

What's your name, please ?

제 이름은 이명호입니다.
Che irŭmŭn Imyŏnghoimnida.

My name is Yi Myong-ho.

또 만날 수 있길 바랍니다.
Tto mannal su itkil paramnida.

I hope we can meet again sometime.

잘 부탁 드립니다.
Chal put'ak tŭrimnida.

Do me a favor.